T0065194

I F   I

H A D   M Y

W I S H

I F I

H A D M Y

W I S H

B A R B A R A R A S M U S S E N

Copyright © 2023 Barbara Rasmussen.

All rights reserved. No part of this book may be used or reproduced by
any means, graphic, electronic, or mechanical, including photocopying,
recording, taping or by any information storage retrieval system
without the written permission of the author except in the case
of brief quotations embodied in critical articles and reviews.

Archway Publishing books may be ordered
through booksellers or by contacting:

Archway Publishing
1663 Liberty Drive
Bloomington, IN 47403
www.archwaypublishing.com
844-669-3957

Because of the dynamic nature of the Internet, any web addresses or
links contained in this book may have changed since publication and
may no longer be valid. The views expressed in this work are solely those
of the author and do not necessarily reflect the views of the publisher,
and the publisher hereby disclaims any responsibility for them.

Any people depicted in stock imagery provided by Getty Images are
models, and such images are being used for illustrative purposes only.
Certain stock imagery © Getty Images.

ISBN: 978-1-6657-5031-8 (sc)
ISBN: 978-1-6657-5030-1 (e)

Library of Congress Control Number: 2023917998

Print information available on the last page.

Archway Publishing rev. date: 09/28/2023

This collection of poems, written along
my journey, is for my daughters.
The lights of my life — the two souls that chose me.

I hope these words inspire, uplift, and give guidance or hope,
because at the end of the day, if I did have my WISH -
I wouldn't change a thing.

If I had my wish…

If I had my wish, would I change course? Would I shift direction?

If I had my wish, would I give up 1,000 little miracles that paved my way; that steered my ship?

If I had my wish, would I forfeit the most important people in my life? Would I risk the gems I found along my way?

I heard another say…
If I had my wish, she'd still be here.
Well, if I had my wish, would I still be there?

If I had my wish… I wouldn't change a thing.

Love Like A Chain

He wrapped his love around me like a chain
Thick and cold
Meant to ensnare like a trap

He said "no one will love you like I do."
I silently prayed he was right.

I broke through that chain
It took nearly all I had to free myself
I can breath now

Is this Love?

He torments me,
       tortures me,
       tries to wear me down.

I say what comes around goes around
       I worry about when his time will come

I walked away
I turned my back
Seeking respect is how I
       justified my flight

Someone now has
       someone that loved me most
Will she ever share in the warmth I once felt?

I doubt their connection
Our bond was strong
He pines for me still
I feel it in his anger and averted eyes

Angry Sea

Up and down
Back and forth
My emotions are as irrational
As an angry sea.

Do I love thee
Do I need thee
Please someone help me

This is Love

One true love in my life
No doubt, no despair
Only endless smiles
And my heart swelling
With joy and contentment

Her hair like mine
Her smile forever bright
Her moods – definitely me
Those amazing brown eyes

I have not failed
I have created a perfect little girl
My serenity

My Path

I constantly question my path
Deliberating which fork to choose
Whether to take the smooth downhill slope
or trek up the rocky incline
always wondering, did I choose the wrong path?

My Path….
Maybe my path is just that
The constant choice
The forks in the road
At times the smooth downhill glide
At times the rugged incline

Maybe my path is to learn from each and every twist and turn
To grow and change on the journey
To constantly be a better version - to make myself a better version
To inspire the little ones I've created

Wrong Heart

Letting someone into my daughter's life –
   Not a wise decision

Letting someone into my daughter's heart –
   Ridiculous mistake

She's so young and trusting,
   But maybe less fragile than I
Maybe I worry about the wrong heart…..

Regret

They say, "I'm so proud!
Look what you've done."
I feel nothing but failure.

They say, "No one else could survive.
You're the only one."
I feel nothing but regret.

They say, "Hold your chin up high.
You've achieved all you've worked for."
I say, "Give me back my life.
I'm sorry I shut the door."

I Sleep

I sleep to forget
I sleep to ease the pain
I sleep to dream
And be happy again
Why have I caused such destruction
Now not just in one but in two
I'll sleep to forget
I'll sleep to ease the pain

Hipocrisy

I am told I am a hypocrite
I suppose I am
I appear completely in control and happy
Ha!

Is it wrong to feign the part?
To play the role?
Is it hypocrisy to hide the pain from the world?

He would rather I fall apart
Break and bend at his knees
Collapse under the pressure
Never!

Suffocating

He said, "I need it right away"
I look back and try not to laugh
"get in line" I feel like shouting
How about a little me first?
I say "I live for my daughter."
Yes
But, I also live for school, work, my family, my bills….
Married – I felt I had no identity
That I could not make decisions
Where my needs were ever a factor
I was forced to live for a unit
That was not even satisfying for me
Then, I felt I could never feel so suffocated, so trapped
How wrong I was!
I have no choices now
I never feel comfortable with my decisions
Second guessing and regret have become my nature
I am slowly suffocating

Tangible Hysteria

I am holding onto the
Tiniest of threads
It is stretched so tight I fear
The snap to come
I am bordering on hysteria
Caused by my extreme anxiety
Is this worth the agony?
Could this possibly be worth the agony?

They say it will all be worth it
That on reflection I will wonder why
I was ever so distraught

I doubt I will ever forget this fear
I fear I will constantly know this torture

Sadly, I believed that writing would help dissipate my anxiety
But it has created a tangible black and white out of the intangible
That moments ago I could ignore

Thin Ice

You tentatively test the surface
It's slippery and dangerous
Yet, exciting and exhilarating at the same time.

You choose to be brave
   To show your strength and resilience
You skate onto the thin ice
   Big smile and open arms

You slip and occasionally fall
But you push on trying to overcome your fears

You start to feel confident, relaxed, safe…
Then it starts
   First, you hear it – that loud slap of a crack
          That heavy sigh as the ice takes a breath
          And starts to give way
          To the turbulent water below
Then, you see it – that razor sharp line
          Carving its way across the pristine surface

You consider staying the course,
Overcoming your fear – proving to all that you can persevere

Do you ignore the cracks?
Do you risk your safety?
Or
Do you cut your losses and head back to the safety of the shore?

A heart breaks like ice
Sometimes it's a long slow razor thin crack
Other times it's a sudden shattering flood that drowns one in an instant

Yet, we continue to test the ice, risk our safety
We fall
We shatter
We break
We get back up
We trust
We fall
We love again

Unhappy ... Again

I was happy
I never thought I could be again
    That I would feel so close
    And have a best friend

It was blissful and all-consuming
    But also devastating to lose

Can one find love once, twice... a third time?

True love should not know this end.

Wait....

Weight
Heavy, solid - almost unbearable

It presses on my chest
As a reminder
I am not ok

I have moments of peace and happiness
When I think I can be strong enough to lift it
But Wait …

Ever-lurking, ever-there
Heavy, solid - almost unbearable
Weight

Flip Flop

I flip and flop

And I flip and flop

> I feel the weight
> Of a pendulum
> Turning over and over
> And over in my mind
> knocking rhythmically on my heart

> It is heavy like a weighted blanket
> Or a stone tied to an ankle

I flip and flop

And I flip and flop

With indecision and confusion and fear
Drowning in despair

The Edge

Standing at the edge
Do I jump off into the unknown
Risk my sanity
Or back away
Stay where it is safe and known

Mother

Mothering comes in many forms
Sometimes you get to choose your family
Made up of those who've supported you,
nurtured you and helped you grow.

Other times, you are forced to walk alone
And seek family at every interaction
hoping for that mothering love
from a friend, a partner, a child even.

A mother's energy can be a beautiful safe haven
Yet, it can also be a web of deception and hurt.
Those caught in the thick toxic sludge that is a jealous mother
fear every twist and turn of life may
shift and catch them off guard
Defensive always they must be.

Yet, some — even without a mother's love
can rise above and BE a mother's love
to all those around them

Shards of glass

Words pierce me like shards of glass.
As I lay there, silent and still, I feel raw as if
skin was being peeled from my bones.

The pain is torturous.
How could someone you love so dearly
inflict such pain with words.

Words with sharp spiny splinters that get under
your skin and are impossible to eradicate.

Eventually, there is the numb as you start to heal.
The wounds are tender and often rebleed
With time and some repression, you ultimately
begin to feel again and timidly trust

But those shards of glass and the splintered pieces remain
Just under the surface.
And with any misstep or side glance
the bleeding may start again.

It's Cold

It's cold
The air I breath is warm and humid
But it's cold

I feel the anxiety creeping
Up my spine like a serpent of pain

I do my best to push it down – keep it at bay
With every deep breath, I shudder with cold
I wear the years of loneliness like a dark, heavy cloak.

I'm not sad or unhappy – just lonely
I want more… better…. always

I don't settle or allow
I don't forgive easily
And, I never forget

Once hurt or wronged in any way,
My dark heavy cloak goes on
So I can't be truly injured

The pain I inflict will be my own doing – not yours

It is cold and this cloak doesn't keep me warm.

And then there were 3

I felt like I needed to run away
> *Hide from it all*
> *Escape*
> *And, so I did*

I ran
I hid
I took a salty breath in the ocean
And gave you the space to exist
> *Free of the drama*
> *Free of the stress*
> *Free of them*

And, exist you did
> *You grew*
> *You flourished*

You clung to me for safety at times, but you ran toward life
> *unafraid   uncluttered   free*
> *All that I wished to be.*

Inspiration

Do I inspire my little ones?
No award or degree can take the place of my greatest achievements

The souls I am lucky enough to call mine.
My family – my unit of three

My ducks in a row
My chicks

I wish to inspire
    I wish to ignite
        I wish to be their Light.

When she cries

When she cries, I cry
When she hurts, I hurt

From before the day of her arrival,
    I could feel and sense every potential pain
As if I knew this cold, dark, and often ugly place
    would scar her time and again.

I try my best to protect her
    To keep her safe and warm with my love.
I build a fortress around her.

Overbearing and consuming at times, she resists and pulls away.

Thankfully, she returns
    knowing she is safe and loved in my arms.

You Laugh

Laughing
Always laughing at me

Why am I so funny?
Why is my path so amusing?

I made mistakes
I stumbled
I fell flat on my face

Still you laugh?

I've raised strong, independent women
    who see this world differently because of me

I helped those in need
    sometimes with just a smile or a kind word
I selflessly loved
    even when I shouldn't have
I stayed the course
    when I should have jumped ship

And still, you laugh

You laugh at my successes
You laugh at my failures
You laugh behind my back and
You laugh in my face

My Cyclical Life

Why this circle never ending
Painful
So bitterly painful

I give and give and give and give
Til exhaustion and sometimes financial drain overcome me

I try to be the best - sister mother daughter friend
I am. I know I am

Yet I am not

It feels like glass on my skin
Blades piercing holes in my heart
A choking grip around my neck

I know I am good
I know I do right
I know I am never what they say

But why do they say?
Why accuse?
Why assault?

Can't they see their own faults?
Must I always rise above?
When will it stop?

I think the answer is in my disconnect.
When they can no longer hurt me, they will stop trying

When the past's unresolved energy
no longer seeps its way into every crack of my life
Like black toxic mold

I will succeed in the disengage
I will be at a place where I can safely say NO MORE!
And go about MY PEACE
This cannot continue

Choosing Chaos

Allow yourself the freedom to feel badly
And recognize that is a great part of who you are

Feel badly
Feel empathy
But do not feel responsible

You are allowed to disconnect
You are allowed to walk your own path
Find your own happiness
Equal at least to those around you

End the patterns that trap and confine
Stop allowing chaos over personal serenity
Choose peace over chaos
Choose YOU!

Good Enough

No one is ever good enough because I was raised to believe that
I am not good enough.
I hold others to an impossible standard that no one can meet.

I am critical because I was criticized.

I expect everyone to fail me because everyone has failed me.
I choose those destined to fail me
Ultimately, I guess there is comfort in the expected

I need to let go
        of criticism
        of judgment
        of chasing failure

I need to make mistakes, learn, grow and move on.

I need to stop demanding perfection and instilling failure.
I am good enough
So are you

Not this …

I know what I do not want
I do not want chaos
I do not want constant upheaval
I do not want to be compared or judged or ridiculed

I do not want to be disrespected
I do not want to be devalued
I do not want to be put third, fourth … thirteenth.
I do not want this
Not this …

The Journey

He said "I want to live more and do less in the time I have left.
LIVE WITH ME!"
Felt like he was asking me to dive head-first into a rocky rapid-
filled current.
Similar to the Great Falls he took me to so long ago

I eased into that water - trepidly, slowly, intentionally.
I cried often - a soul-draining type of cry that left me exhausted
for days.

What choice did I have?
Could I turn my back on someone so endearing, so sweet, so
harmless and leave him alone in this.
At times his anxiety and fear were palpable
Something I could feel, touch, smell in the air

Deep within me, I knew it wasn't a choice I could ever make.

I help people.
I solve problems.
That's just who I am.

I am a fixer.
If not a fixer, I am a soother and a healer.

Instead of seriously considering walking away, I chose instead to
listen to the voice in my dream.
I envisioned a clear crystal cylinder surrounding my entire being.
This invisible cylinder was my protection from all the toxic energy
that was sure to flow from him and
    try to seep into my core.
I used this cylinder to protect myself
    to stay clear-minded and surrounded by positivity.

I thought if I could keep this unbreakable crystal-clear cylinder
intact and around me at virtually all
    times, I would be able to do what he asked.
I would be able to live with him for the time he had left.

And so began our journey.

It's not you,
it's not me, it's us

It is not personal
I want more, different, less, something similar
I want to be a priority

I tried to change
I tried to abide
Now, I must accept

I cannot change you
I cannot change me
I tried to understand
    to fit your mold
    to mold you into me
Left us both broken

Instead, I will meet you with understanding
I will stop over-looking what I know to be true

I will release you
I will release myself
I will give us peace

We have a pattern of incompatibility
I will honor this pain and let it go

I will let you go

Life in Rewind

Living a life on play back
Constantly reversing, looking back

It is no way to be
No way to get ahead, to move forward

Life in rewind is not a good life
It is days of endless regret and indecision

Rip the cassette tape out of the player
Smash the CD
Scratch the vinyl
Play a new tune and stop the rewind

Betrayal

My eyes betray me
They fly open at the crack of dawn

I know I need to rest
   but even if I force them closed,
My eyes they betray me.

My eyes play a continuous reel of the past
   Reminding me of what I've lost

I try to play tricks on my mind's video replay
I convince myself of all I've gained in the process
Willing myself to see the positive – to see the light

But my eyes – they know
They won't be closed – shut off to reality

They know the truth
They know the pain
They've seen what my mind and heart try to deny.

My eyes betray me

Balloon

Sometimes I am
bright, colorful, buoyant
Filled with fresh air and vibrancy
Soaring through a bright beautiful blue sky.
Other times I am deflated, shriveled, torn to bits
Slowly losing altitude and descending back to reality
being pulled down by the strong force of gravity
Tied to a string I cannot rid myself of
Choking, struggling, gasping while
All remaining air dissipates.

Consistency

He has consistently been no good
He has repeatedly failed to heal my broken
He has abandoned the little girl in me that needs love and protection

He has continually put me in a place of needing strength
    Forcing me to trudge forward alone

I am allowed to end this cycle
I am allowed to protect the little girl inside of me over him
I am allowed to seek what is missing

And be grateful for his consistency

Crumbled

Clean white unblemised
Sheet of finest paper
What secrets do you hold?
What will you unfold?

Harsh dark writing stains the page
Rips holes into the linen flesh
What torment must the author feel?
Why punish the pages so grippingly?

Crumbled and tossed aside
An idea not fully formed
A forgotten thought

This is how it feels.
This is how you make me feel.
Used and crumbled and tossed aside

Others' Pain

Others' pain
Another's trouble
Always center stage

My fears
My sadness
Rarely the main event

Invisible Bars

These invisible bars like a prison surround me
no one can see - only me

These invisible bars like a prison that cage me
thwarted at every attempt to flee

Meant to keep me safe yet often keep me hostage

Unable to spread my wings and fly
I fear I will wither and die

Ties that bind

Ties that bind us
Strong and unbreakable

Some will last
And withstand time

Others will be stretched so thin
They may snap or become brittle

Those that retain their strength
Will become the hammock on
Which we may rest a lifetime

My Turn

I finally get to choose
Myself
Not another

I choose a new start
A new place of anonymity
Where I can fully bloom

Free from my past at every intersection
Reminders in every local face

I get to have newness
People who just see me
Not the stories they've heard
Or the other people they know who've heard something
… anything … nonsense

It will be freeing
Like flying
Like getting to choose

I'm excited.
I am happy
I am loved and I love
MYSELF

Change

Slow like a rusted pocket watch whose gears barely move
Or quick like shifting gears in a speeding sportscar

Change happens
Whether we are ready or willing
Change is a part of our existence
Without it, our spirit cannot grow, expand, or fully realize its potential

Change is necessary

The rust must give way for those gears to turn and move

Pause

Pause … interesting word.
Even saying it makes you slow down.
Being child of alcoholics, I'm not good with sitting in
silence …taking time … pausing.

I'm a fixer, a mover, a doer.
I distract.
I keep myself busy.
I wasn't taught to sit with my thoughts.
I was raised to hide, to cover up, to pretend, to make everything
look shiny on the outside.

When I look back, I see the pain I inflicted on myself and others
by not PAUSING
By refusing the slow.
Now, I will force myself to PAUSE.
I will force myself to mourn all of my past.
I will sit with it ALL.

I do know that unless I walk through the pain and feel the sorrow
and accept the loss,
I will never truly move forward.
I will never truly be content unless I *PAUSE*.

Alone

Thought I would be sad
Thought I would be afraid
Thought I would feel regret - despair even

I do not.

Alone – I feel content
      I feel proud
      I feel ready

I did a great job!
I brought a beautiful soul into this world – twice!
I cared and aided and assisted others.
I selflessly sacrificed for years.

I was rarely alone.
I had no space for just me.
I relished in the company and appreciated every moment

But now, I am ALONE
And, I am not sad
I am not afraid
I do not feel regret or despair

I am LIGHT.

Peace

I can be at peace
I can stop running from
Running away
Running toward

I can exhale
I am safe
My people are safe

Him

Dumpy bar
Walked in late
Disheveled without a care never expecting him

I looked up and locked eyes
It hit me like a jolt
Never ever have I felt such
Instant connection such a strong pull

I dismissed it in my mind, but my heart pulled.
We talked. We listened. We lingered.
He grabbed my hand while walking, and there it was again
        that jolt - that connection – that pull
Like an invisible rope … thick and heavy tying us together but
light and freeing like silk thread
A beautiful web ensnaring us both.

Tapestry

When I close my eyes
I see the tapestry of my life.
It's woven with colors and vines and flowers and birds.
It does not make me anxious.
It does not make me cry.
I see each peace throughout the twists and
turns in the jungle that is life.
I have created a beautiful tapestry that
I can look back on and smile

Time

I used my moments wisely
   Gathered minutes up like seeds
   Then planted those specs of time to create beautiful flowers
   of every color.

When I look back over my time,
   I see a vibrant kaleidoscope of color

All those seeds turned to flowers turned to color turned to light

I am proud of my time garden

I used my moments wisely
   and now there is a heavenly rainbow of color
   trailing behind me for all to enjoy

Tree

I am a tree
My roots are strong and steady
My trunk is solid
My bark is thick and protective
When my branches crack and fall, others spring to life
My bough provides rest and shade
I nourish those around me with my energy
I dispense all negativity into the deep earth where
it cannot escape and cause more harm
Solid
Steady
Protective

Puppy Love

Those endearing eyes
Those soulful stares
The excitement when you return
The whimper when you leave
Her prancing around your garden
Her barking to protect you
The unconditional love found nowhere but here
In her loving snuggle and her sigh of relief at the end of the day

It's All BS

It is what it is
You will know when you know

Stop the madness
Who ever really knows

We are creatures of habit
We aim to conform

It isn't what it isn't
You will never know

Pennies

See a penny, pick it up
Pennies found
Pennies lost
Penny in my dead father's pocket now glued to a frame

Little messages from him I've convinced myself
So I collect these treasures and store them in jars
My pennies from a life stolen too soon

Wishing

Wishing on a star
Blowing out a candle
Tossing a penny into a pond

We wish
We hope
We test fate

Sometimes that star burns out
That candle melts onto the cake
That penny misses the mark

We forget to have faith
We lose hope
We test fate

We forget to keep wishing … KEEP WISHING!

Printed in the United States
by Baker & Taylor Publisher Services